THE COMPLETE ASIAN KOSHER COOKBOOK

WINNING RECIPES OF AUTHENTIC ASIAN CUISINE

SHIFRAH DEVORAH WITT AND ZIPPORAH MALKA HELLER

First published 2010
Copyright © 2010 by Shifrah Devorah Witt and Zipporah Malka Heller
ISBN 978-1-56871-544-5

Published and distributed by:
TARGUM PRESS, INC.
22700 W. Eleven Mile Rd.
Southfield, MI 48034
E-mail: targum@targum.com
Fax: 888-298-9992
www.targum.com

DEDICATION

To kosher cooks everywhere, who love to experiment and try new things. May this book inspire you and nourish your families.

And to my wonderfully sensitive daughter, Shifrah Devorah, who has been my partner in the adventure of exploring the world of Asian food since she was two years old.

Zipporah Malka Heller

To Yedidya, my incredible husband, and Menachem Mendel, our sweet son. There are no words for the joy the two of you bring to my life. I am forever grateful to both of you. Thank you for being exactly who you are. May we grow as a family from strength to strength and build a true *bayis ne'eman b'Yisrael, ad meah v'esrim.*

And to my mother, co-author, and best friend, Zipporah Malka Heller, for being my partner in this book and in all my endeavors. For all the Asian food over all the years. Most of my happiest memories growing up are eating Asian food with you.

Shifrah Devorah Witt

ACKNOWLEDGMENTS

With gratitude to Hashem, for His kindness in all aspects of our lives and specifically in allowing us to write this book.

To the amazing staff of Targum for their enthusiastic support and assistance. To Esther Heller who saw what this book could be — thank you for helping us actualize this dream into a reality. To Chaya Baila Gavant for your patience and vision, to Bracha David who tirelessly input corrections and checked and rechecked this manuscript, and to Malka Turner — you are the most incredible copy editors we've ever worked with. Thank you for your expert eyes and diligence. To Gittel Kaplan for the beautiful typesetting, to Michal Eisikowitz for your work on the back cover, and to the gifted graphics artist Beena Sklare, who brought our recipes to life through her beautiful graphics and her kind heart. We cannot thank you enough.

Shifrah Devorah and Zipporah Malka

To my mother Bertha Heller, a.k.a. Bubbie, whose Sweet and Sour Chicken inspired us. To my dad, Seymour Heller, *zt"l*, who introduced me to Chinese food and my love for it. To Uncle Seymour Lublin, for taking me to my first Chinese restaurants when I was a child in Detroit. To my cousin, Jill Lublin, for introducing me to Thai food. And for Andy Kan who taught my dad to make flawless rice. To Wanda Graham, for helping me find my first egg roll recipe. To Dawn McDuffie, friend of a lifetime, for all of your help getting this book through the final stages. To Janet Weiner, one of our dearest friends — this book literally couldn't have happened without you. To Yedidya Witt, son-in-law extraordinaire, for being so adventurous and loving our experiments, and to Menachem Mendel, my grandson, for loving Asian food at only thirteen months old, trying all of our recipes, loving tofu, being able to say it, and learning to use chopsticks at fourteen and a half months while we were in the final stages of writing this book.

Zipporah Malka

And to our Shabbos guests for their encouragement and appreciation. And to my father Gary I. Frank, who took me to countless Asian restaurants growing up, introducing me to sukiyaki, sushi, and Chinese chicken noodle soup. And to my wonderful grandparents, Bubbie Heller and Janice and Warren Frank. Thank you all — this book happened because of you.

Shifrah Devorah

CONTENTS

CHINESE

JAPANESE

THAI

CHINA

No one knows why Jews love Chinese food, but here is our theory: The Chinese food that came to America was food meant for a king. Isn't that what we prepare for Shabbos? There are many types of regional cooking in China, and we showcased as many as possible to give you a variety of options, from the spicy to the subtle. Chinese food is healthy, flavorful, and delicious.

JAPAN

The Japanese have taken their small amount of land abutting the ocean and harvested the best it has to offer. Sushi, a trademark Japanese food, has become a favorite in many Jewish communities worldwide. Complete with iodine-rich seaweed, omega-3–rich fish, and vitamin-packed vegetables, Japanese food is probably the lowest in fat and most dietetic of all Asian foods. On top of its health benefits, Japanese food is light and fresh.

THAILAND

Thai food combines unusual ingredients to create delectable dishes. From coconut milk, fresh basil, and cumin to peanut butter, rice noodles, and crushed chili peppers, there is a surprise in every bite. As Thai food doesn't rely heavily on soy sauce, it can be prepared for those on a low-sodium diet. Although we've left out the recipes using more exotic and difficult-to-find spices, we've recreated the flavors of the Thai kitchen and brought it to yours.

ASIAN CUISINE

PHILIPPINES

Filipino cuisine blends multiple cultures. Its food is influenced by the Spanish, native Filipinos, and Asian cuisine. Emerging with its own unique taste, the food is simple, interesting, and surprisingly easy to prepare. When you are in the mood for something new, give it a try. You won't be disappointed.

SOUTHEAST ASIA
(INDONESIA, MALAYSIA, VIETNAM)

Here is a cacophony of flavors brought together by neighboring countries and European influences. The flavors of Southeast Asia create a fusion of spices, textures, and colors sure to enhance your culinary experience. Through its use of ingredients such as five-spice powder, cellophane noodles, and turmeric, the tastes of Indonesia, Malaysia, and Vietnam are some of the less often visited but most satisfying in Asian cooking.

INDIA

Perfect for, but certainly not limited to, the vegetarian, Indian food is known for its aromatic flavors and spices. Curry, the most well-known Indian seasoning, is both spicy and sweet. While many of these dishes can be served together to make an even more spectacular meal, they are each wonderful on their own. Indian cuisine is one of the only Asian cuisines that include cooked fruit as part of the meal.

TIPS AND TRICKS FOR ASIAN COOKING

Welcome to the wonderful world of Asian cooking! We're so glad you're here. We've discovered that Asian cooking can be one of the most exciting, enjoyable, and fulfilling types of cooking there is. And believe us, we've tried them all. We always find that there is no feeling like preparing a delicious Asian dinner and knowing that our favorite restaurant couldn't have done it any better.

Though at first glance Asian cooking may seem intimidating, we've tried to simplify our recipes without compromising authenticity or taste. We've also found that being prepared is the key to an enjoyable cooking experience. Once you get the hang of our tricks and tips for Asian cooking, you'll be whipping up five-course sheva berachos extravaganzas, or making simple soups at a moment's notice just because you or your family are in the mood for Asian. Enjoy the cooking, enjoy eating what you've created, but most of all enjoy the process.

Best wishes,
Shifrah Devorah and Zipporah Malka

Make sure your kitchen is stocked with basics like tofu, chicken breasts, sugar, a selection of rice and rice noodles, garlic, ginger, low-sodium soy sauce, and sesame oil. Fresh vegetables are a must.

with Asian cooking takes a bit longer than other cuisine, but the actual cooking time is normally very quick, so in the end things even out.

so you don't get surprised or miss a step in the middle.

on-hand before you start. We like to put everything out on the counter so the ingredients are handy when we need them.

in all of our recipes. If you do choose regular soy sauce, reduce the amount you put into the recipe or your dish will be too salty.

we use organic unrefined sugar instead of white sugar in all our recipes. It works well and offers lots of health benefits. If you choose to use white sugar, you may want to use a little less than the amount we suggest.

We suggest using canola oil, but you may substitute peanut oil in Chinese cooking as well. Never substitute olive oil. The flavor is too strong, and it will affect the taste of the dish.

The Asian method of stir-frying, or cooking quickly over a high heat, allows the vegetables to retain their beautiful bright colors and most of their natural vitamins. When cooking, add your firmer vegetables to the dish first. If a dish is going to sit on a *blech* or be reheated, make sure to undercook the vegetables.

Rice noodles and mung bean noodles are soaked in warm water for thirty minutes and then added toward the end of the cooking, once the vegetables or meat have already been cooked. Always taste the noodles to make sure they are actually cooked through. These noodles are fun to eat and a welcome change from the usual wheat alternative.

and adding them to the dish toward the end of the cooking time to thicken it and make a nice gravy. It's important to stir the dish constantly after adding the cornstarch so the mixture doesn't get lumpy. Taste the dish before serving it. If it tastes like cornstarch, lower the heat and stir until the taste goes away, three to five minutes.

Even though these recipes have been tested and retested, each brand of soy sauce is a little different, as are the flavors of the veggies, meats, and noodles. Do a quick taste test and see if you need a little extra sugar, salt, or soy sauce. Tastes are highly individual, and this is your opportunity to make our dish yours.

You'll eat slower, allowing more time for digestion, and they add an authentic feel. If you are serving Asian food for Shabbos or Yom Tov, make sure to separate your chopsticks in advance.

ITEMS TO KEEP ON HAND

UTENSILS

- large frying pan with a lid
- large spatula for stir-frying
- long tongs or slotted spoon for deep-frying

FRESH ITEMS

- chicken thighs
- chicken wings
- boneless chicken breasts
- cut up steak or stir-fry beef
- 2 packages of tofu (this doesn't freeze well — only keep on hand if you intend to use within a week)
- fresh garlic
- fresh ginger
- cilantro
- green onions
- fresh mushrooms
- bean sprouts
- white onions

IN YOUR CABINET

- cornstarch
- flour
- organic unrefined sugar
- low-sodium soy sauce
- canola oil
- sesame oil
- canned coconut milk
- rice vinegar
- white vinegar
- mirin (sweet seasoning sauce)
- wasabi powder
- dry English mustard
- Chinese five-spice powder
- Indian curry powder
- crushed red pepper flakes
- egg roll wrappers
- wonton wrappers
- spring roll wrappers
- jasmine rice
- basmati rice
- white rice
- sushi rice
- powdered chicken soup mix
- cellophane or mung bean noodles
- wide rice noodles
- vermicelli rice noodles
- spaghetti or capellini noodles
- sesame seeds

TEAS

- jasmine
- oolong
- Lipton
- ginger
- green tea
- chai

CHINESE

FAST AND EASY EGG ROLLS Ⓟ

These egg rolls are so good you may be full before you get to the main course.

16 spring roll or egg roll wrappers

canola oil, for frying

FILLING

2 tablespoons canola oil

8 cups shredded cabbage and carrot mix

2 cups bean sprouts

4 green onions, thinly sliced

½ teaspoon salt

Heat 2 tablespoons oil in pan on medium high. Add cabbage and carrot mix and cook for 1 minute. Add bean spouts and green onions and cook for another minute. Add salt. Remove from pan and cool.

Lay 1 wrapper on a flat plate. Keep other wrappers covered so they won't dry out. Place 2–3 tablespoons of filling onto bottom third of wrapper. Fold both right and left side of wrapper in towards the middle, then roll to top. Fry seam-side down in 1½ inches of hot oil over medium heat. Turn over and fry on other side.

Yields 16 egg rolls.

DIPPING SAUCES FOR EGG ROLLS Ⓟ

A sweet addition to the egg rolls above.

SWEET AND SOUR SAUCE

8 tablespoons strawberry jam (or plum or orange marmalade)

8 tablespoons white vinegar

Mix together jam and vinegar. Serve over egg rolls with a dab of hot mustard.

HOT MUSTARD

4 tablespoons dry English mustard

5 tablespoons plus 1 teaspoon water

Mix mustard with water. Dab on egg rolls and serve with Sweet and Sour Sauce.

BOILED OR FRIED WONTONS

Whether you like your wontons in soup, boiled with dipping sauce, or as a fried appetizer, this recipe will have your crowd coming back for more.

½ large chicken breast, cut into ¾-inch pieces

1 teaspoon cornstarch

2 teaspoons water

1 package circular wonton wrappers (20 wrappers)

canola oil, for frying

Combine cornstarch and water and coat chicken pieces with mixture. Place 1 piece of chicken in the middle of a wonton wrapper. Dab a little water along edge of wrapper and fold into a half-circle. Seal edges together. Dab water along outside edges and pinch the two sides of the half-circle together. If this is too challenging or you are in a hurry, leave them as half-circles.

For boiled wontons: Boil wontons in soup until they are translucent and chicken is no longer pink on the inside, approximately 5–7 minutes. Open one to check if it is fully cooked.

If you are not serving the wontons immediately, remove from soup until ready to serve. Don't overcook!

For fried wontons: Heat a medium-size frying pan over medium-high heat. Add oil ½ inch deep. Fry wontons in oil until golden on outside and chicken is no longer pink on inside. Watch carefully, as they cook quickly.
Serve with dipping sauce.

Yields 20 wontons. Serves 5 as an appetizer.

SOY AND VINEGAR DIPPING SAUCE

4 tablespoons vinegar

4 tablespoons low-sodium soy sauce

Mix vinegar and soy sauce together and serve.

Makes enough for 10–20 wontons.

POT STICKERS ▣

Also known as Chinese dumplings, pot stickers resemble fried kreplach. Kids love them.

25 circular wonton wrappers

canola oil, for frying

3 tablespoons water

FILLING

½ pound ground beef

1 tablespoon sesame oil

1 tablespoon low-sodium soy sauce

¼ teaspoon salt, optional

1 green onion, diced

2 teaspoons ginger, diced

2 teaspoons fresh garlic, diced

Mix filling ingredients together thoroughly in a large bowl. Place 1 teaspoon of filling in the center of a wonton wrapper. Fold wrapper in half. Using a little water, gently run your finger along the edge of the wrapper to seal. Sit the wrappers up on a plate as you finish.

To fry, heat 2 tablespoons oil in a frying pan over medium-low heat. Place pot stickers in pan. Fry on each side until lightly browned (1–2 minutes). Carefully add water to pan and immediately cover with a tight lid. Wait until water is completely absorbed (2–3 minutes). Open 1 pot sticker to make sure meat is cooked thoroughly. If it's not, add a small amount of water and cook an additional 1–2 minutes. Serve with Spicy Soy Dipping Sauce or Peanut Butter Dipping Sauce (see page 17).

Yields 25 pot stickers.

SPICY SOY DIPPING SAUCE ⅅ

Mildly spicy, and oh so good!

½ teaspoon crushed red pepper flakes

2 tablespoons low-sodium soy sauce

2 teaspoons white or rice vinegar

1 teaspoon green onion, thinly sliced

2 teaspoons sugar, optional

¼ teaspoon sesame oil, optional

Mix crushed red pepper flakes, soy sauce, vinegar, green onion, sugar, and sesame oil. Sprinkle with additional green onions, and serve as a wonderful dipping sauce for wontons or pot stickers.

Makes enough for 10–20 wontons.

CHILI OIL DIPPING SAUCE ⅅ

Hot, hot, hot!

4 tablespoons canola oil

2 tablespoons small whole dried chili peppers

Heat oil in a pan. Add chili peppers. Cook over low heat until peppers begin to brown. Remove from heat and let stand for a few minutes. Discard peppers and use oil as a dipping sauce or to add a little spice to any dish, or add a few drops to Soy and Vinegar Dipping Sauce (see page 15) and serve with pot stickers.

Makes enough for 10–20 wontons.

PEANUT BUTTER DIPPING SAUCE ⅅ

This creamy sauce is delicious.

2 tablespoons creamy peanut butter

¼ teaspoon sesame oil

½ teaspoon crushed red pepper flakes

2 teaspoons low-sodium soy sauce

1 teaspoon white or rice vinegar

3 tablespoons water

Mix all ingredients together. Serve as dipping sauce for wontons or pot stickers.

Makes enough for 10–20 wontons.

CHINESE

GROUND BEEF IN LETTUCE CUPS M

This dish is easy to make and fun to eat. It's also low in calories, making it very diet friendly.

1 pound lean ground beef

2 tablespoons canola oil

1 cup frozen peas

1 cup fried vermicelli rice noodles (see page 20), optional

8–10 large lettuce leaves, whole (romaine or butter lettuce)

MARINADE

5 cloves garlic, finely chopped

1 tablespoon blackstrap molasses

2 teaspoons low-sodium soy sauce

2 teaspoons dry red wine

⅛ teaspoon freshly ground black pepper

3 tablespoons water

Combine ingredients for marinade. Add ground beef and let marinate for 15 minutes. In a large frying pan, heat oil. Add marinated meat and stir-fry on a high heat until meat is cooked through. Add frozen peas and cook for 1 more minute. Turn off heat and stir in fried rice noodles. Remove mixture to a serving platter and serve next to lettuce leaves to be used as wraps. Place a lettuce leaf on your plate, spoon meat into center, and fold up lettuce to form a cup.

Serves 4–6.

CHINESE CHICKEN SALAD

This is great for a party where you want the food to show you care. The fried noodles make this an elegant salad.

2 boneless, skinless chicken breasts, cut into ½-inch strips

8 cups shredded lettuce

3 green onions, thinly sliced

2 cups bean sprouts

8 mushrooms, sliced ¼-inch thick

3 carrots, sliced

1–2 tablespoon canola oil

4 cups fried vermicelli rice noodles (see page 20), or 1 5-ounce can fried chow mein noodles

½ cup toasted peanuts

4 tablespoons cilantro

1 4-ounce can mandarin oranges, drained, optional

½ cup dried cranberries, optional

MARINADE

1 teaspoon cornstarch

2 teaspoons dry sherry

2 teaspoons water

pinch freshly ground black pepper

Mix together marinade ingredients. Add chicken strips and marinate 15–30 minutes. Meanwhile, combine lettuce with onions, bean sprouts, mushrooms, and carrots in a large salad bowl.

When chicken is marinated, heat frying pan over medium heat. Add 1–2 tablespoons oil to lightly coat bottom of pan. Add chicken and stir-fry 3–5 minutes until chicken is nicely browned and no longer pink on the inside. Let cool.

Add chicken to salad bowl. Top with fried vermicelli rice noodles, peanuts, cilantro, mandarin oranges, and dried cranberries. Top with Chinese Chicken Salad Dressing (see page 20) and serve.

Serves 4–6.

CHINESE CHICKEN SALAD DRESSING ⓓ

I like to make extra and keep this dressing on hand in the fridge. It is great for pouring over leftover cold pasta for a quick lunch.

¼ cup canola oil

¼ cup rice vinegar

4½ tablespoons sugar

pinch fresh ground black pepper

1 teaspoon toasted sesame seeds (see page 21)

2 teaspoons low-sodium soy sauce

½ teaspoon sesame oil, optional

1 tablespoon chopped fresh cilantro, optional

Mix all ingredients and pour over Chinese Chicken Salad (see page 19).

FRIED VERMICELLI RICE NOODLES ⓓ

These delicious fried noodles are a wonderful addition to a salad. Just be careful when you are cooking them, as they cook quickly and can burn easily.

2 handfuls vermicelli rice noodles, cut into 3–4-inch pieces

canola oil, for frying

In a deep pot with high sides, preheat 3–4 inches of oil over medium heat. Add 1 noodle to test if oil is hot enough. The noodle will puff immediately and turn white, floating to the surface. Add a handful of noodles to oil. Turn noodles over immediately to cook on second side for another second. Remove from oil and drain on paper towel. Repeat process. Noodles will keep in refrigerator for up to a week in a sealed container.

Yields 2–3 cups noodles.

ASIAN SALAD ▣

*You can be as creative as you want with this salad.
Mix and match, as you like.*

3 cups shredded lettuce or fresh
spinach

3 cups shredded red cabbage

1 cup bean sprouts

1 green onion, sliced

2 carrots, sliced

3 mushrooms, sliced (button,
fresh shiitake, or portobello)

1 cup Asian Salad Dressing (see
opposite)

¼–½ cup raw or toasted nuts
(peanuts, almonds, cashews,
or walnuts)

2 tablespoons toasted sesame
seeds (see below)

1 cup fried vermicelli rice
noodles (see page 20)

Combine lettuce, cabbage, bean
sprouts, green onion, carrots,
and mushrooms. Toss with Asian
Salad Dressing. Top with nuts,
toasted sesame seeds, and fried
vermicelli rice noodles.

Serves 6–8.

TOASTED SESAME SEEDS ▣

These will intensify the flavor of any dish.

½ cup white sesame seeds

Heat sesame seeds over medium-
low heat in a small dry frying
pan. Stir constantly until seeds
become fragrant and slightly

golden brown. Remove from
heat. Store unused portion in
freezer for up to 2 months.

*Yields eight 1-tablespoon servings, or two
¼-cup servings.*

ASIAN SALAD DRESSING ▣

Easy and delicious.

⅔ cup canola oil

⅓ cup rice vinegar or white
vinegar

4 tablespoons low-sodium soy
sauce

4 tablespoons sugar, optional

2 teaspoons toasted sesame seeds

dash sesame oil, optional

Mix ingredients together. Pour
over salad and enjoy! Store in an
airtight container.

Makes enough for 1 recipe Asian Salad.

DRY TOASTED NUTS ▣

Toasting nuts enhances their natural flavor.

1 cup nuts (peanuts, slivered
almonds, walnuts, or
cashews)

1 teaspoon canola oil, optional

Fry nuts with or without oil in
a small frying pan until nuts

begin to brown and are slightly
fragrant. Remove from heat immediately.

Use as garnish for salads or stir-
fried dishes.

Yields four ¼-cup servings.

CHINESE CHICKEN SOUP

*Also known as Jewish penicillin. The garlic works as a natural antibiotic.
This soup will have everyone feeling great, whether they are sick or not.*

1 large chicken

10 cloves garlic, sliced

3 tablespoons fresh ginger, chopped

1 cup cilantro

8 green onions, whole

water, to cover chicken

1–2 teaspoons sesame oil

dash low-sodium soy sauce, optional

Place chicken, garlic, ginger, cilantro, and green onions in a large pot. Cover with water and bring to a boil. Cook over medium heat, uncovered, 3–5 hours. Taste soup and add sesame oil and a dash of soy sauce to taste. Remove chicken, green onions, and cilantro to a separate container. Strain stock. Serve as is, or use as a base for Wonton Soup (see page 24), or stock for gravy in stir-fried dishes. May be stored in freezer for up to 2 months.

Serves 6–8.

PAREVE CHICKEN SOUP D

Very easy and very versatile.

8 cups hot water plus 8 teaspoons pareve chicken soup mix, prepared according to package directions

8 cloves garlic, sliced

1–2 tablespoons fresh ginger, chopped

1 green onion, sliced

1–2 tablespoons low-sodium soy sauce, optional

1 teaspoon sesame oil

In a saucepan, heat water and pareve chicken soup mix. Add remaining ingredients and bring to a boil.

Serves 6.

EGG DROP SOUP M/D

This soup is great for nights you think you're out of everything. Keep some eggs and a can of corn in stock and watch your kids' faces light up when you serve them this fun-to-eat soup.

4 cups chicken soup stock, or 4 cups water plus 4 teaspoons pareve chicken soup mix, prepared according to package directions

4 teaspoons low-sodium soy sauce

1½ cups canned corn

4 eggs, beaten

Bring chicken soup stock to a boil. Add soy sauce and corn. Bring soup to a full boil and turn off heat. Drizzle beaten egg into hot soup from a height of 7–10 inches above soup, stirring constantly. The egg will form strings and become egg drop soup.

Serves 4–6.

WONTON SOUP  M

Possibly my favorite soup in the world.

8 cups Chinese chicken soup
stock (see page 22)

½ cup raw chicken, diced

1 tablespoon cornstarch, mixed
with 1 tablespoon water

2 mushrooms, thinly sliced

1 carrot, thinly sliced

16 wontons (see page 15)

1 green onion, finely chopped,
for garnish

1 teaspoon sesame oil

sprinkle of cilantro, for garnish

Coat chicken with cornstarch and water mixture. Set aside. Bring chicken soup stock to a boil over high heat. Add chicken, mushrooms, carrot, and wontons, and cook 4–7 minutes. Add green onion, sesame oil, and cilantro. Cook 1–2 minutes and serve.

Serves 8.

HOT AND SOUR SOUP M/D

Unusually delicious. This soup takes only minutes to prepare.

4 cups chicken soup stock, or 4 cups water plus 4 teaspoons pareve chicken soup mix, prepared according to package directions

1 tablespoon dry sherry

1 tablespoon plus 2 teaspoons white vinegar

2 teaspoons low-sodium soy sauce

1 teaspoon sesame oil

½ teaspoon white pepper

½ cup sliced bamboo shoots

½ cup sliced fresh mushrooms (shiitake or button), optional

8 ounces firm tofu, cut into ½-inch strips or cubes

2 tablespoons cornstarch plus 2 tablespoons water, for thickening

1 egg, beaten

2 green onions, sliced into 2-inch pieces

Bring chicken soup stock to a boil. Add dry sherry, vinegar, soy sauce, sesame oil, and pepper, and stir. Add bamboo shoots, mushrooms, and tofu. Add cornstarch and water mixture, stirring constantly to thicken soup. Bring soup to a full boil and then shut off heat. Immediately pour egg into soup from a height of 7–10 inches above pot, stirring soup in figure eights. Add green onions and serve immediately.

Serves 4.

PAREVE CHICKEN NOODLE SOUP WITH TOFU D

This makes a great weeknight dinner when you have no time to cook.

8–10 cups water plus 8–10 teaspoons pareve chicken soup mix, prepared according to package directions

5 cloves garlic, sliced

3–5 slices ginger, optional

2 zucchini, sliced lengthwise and cut in quarters

1 carrot, sliced

1 16-ounce package tofu, cut into small cubes

4 green onions, diced

1 teaspoon sesame oil, optional

1 16-ounce package spaghetti noodles, cooked al dente and drained

Heat water and chicken soup mix. Add garlic, ginger, zucchini, and carrot and cook until tender, approximately 5–10 minutes. Five minutes before serving, add tofu, green onions, and sesame oil. Let soup boil for a few minutes. Add noodles just before serving and heat thoroughly. Serve hot and enjoy!

Serves 6–8.

KUNG PAO CHICKEN

This spicy dish is perfect for those who can't get enough hot food.

2 pounds chicken breasts, cut
    into bite-size pieces

3 tablespoons canola oil

6–10 whole tiny chili peppers

1 cup salted peanuts, skinned

3 teaspoons ginger, minced

3 teaspoons garlic, minced

4 green onions, cut into
    1½-inch pieces

2 tablespoons cornstarch plus
    2 tablespoons water, for
    thickening

MARINADE

2 tablespoons canola oil

2 tablespoons dry sherry

2 tablespoons cornstarch

¼ teaspoon salt

¼ teaspoon white pepper

COOKING SAUCE

4 tablespoons low-sodium soy sauce

2 tablespoons rice vinegar

2 tablespoons dry sherry

½ cup water

1 tablespoon plus 1 teaspoon sugar

Mix together marinade ingredients. Coat chicken with mixture and let sit 15–20 minutes. Combine cooking sauce ingredients and set aside. In a frying pan, heat peppers and peanuts in 1 tablespoon oil and stir-fry until peppers begin to darken. Remove peppers and peanuts and set aside. Add 2 more tablespoons of oil to the pan, plus ginger and garlic, and stir. Add chicken and stir-fry until lightly browned. (Add a little more oil if chicken sticks to pan.) Return peanuts and peppers to pan. Add cooking sauce and green onions. Bring to a boil. Stir cornstarch mixed with water into sauce until thickened.

Serves 4–6.

Note: If possible, remove chili peppers from chicken before serving.

BUBBIE'S SWEET-AND-SOUR CHICKEN ◼

This is an adaptation of Bubbie Heller's famous sweet-and-sour chicken. She used to serve it for company, and to this day she's still getting rave reviews.

3 chicken breasts, cut into 2-inch cubes

canola oil, for deep-frying

STIR-FRIED VEGETABLES

2 tablespoons canola oil

¼ pound fresh mushrooms, cut into quarters

1 red pepper, cut into large chunks

1 green pepper, cut into large chunks

1 onion, cut into large chunks

1 20-ounce can pineapple chunks (1½ cups), juice reserved

1 tomato, cut into eighths

SWEET AND SOUR SAUCE

1½ cups pineapple juice from pineapple chunks

1 cup white vinegar

4 teaspoons low-sodium soy sauce

1¼ cups sugar

½ cup water

4 tablespoons cornstarch, plus 4 tablespoons water, for thickening

BATTER

1 cup flour

1 cup water

⅓ cup cornstarch

½ teaspoon salt

¾ teaspoon baking soda

To prepare vegetables, heat a large frying pan over medium heat. Add 2 tablespoons oil. Stir-fry mushrooms, peppers, onions, and pineapple until onion is slightly translucent. Add tomato, and cook additional 1–2 minutes. Remove from pan and set aside.

To prepare sauce, combine pineapple juice, vinegar, soy sauce, sugar, and water. Bring to a low boil over a medium-high heat. Mix together cornstarch and water and slowly add to sauce, stirring constantly until thickened. Add stir-fried vegetables. Remove from heat and set aside.

Combine ingredients for batter. Stir until the mixture reaches a smooth consistency.

Heat oil 2 inches deep in frying pan over medium-high heat. Dip chicken in batter and deep-fry in oil until brown. Using a slotted spoon, remove chicken to a platter covered with paper towel.

Reheat sauce thoroughly. Serve over chicken and rice.

Serves 6.

Note: If you are in a hurry, you can use bottled Chinese sweet and sour sauce.

CHINESE BAKED CHICKEN Ⓜ

A wonderful dish for an elegant Shabbos meal.

1 large chicken, cut into eighths

MARINADE

¼ cup low-sodium soy sauce

1 tablespoon powdered ginger

1 tablespoon powdered garlic

½ cup water

2 tablespoons sugar

Preheat oven to 350°. Combine soy sauce, ginger, garlic, water, and sugar in a bowl. Add chicken and marinate 30 minutes or longer if time permits. Transfer to a baking pan and bake for 60–90 minutes or until no longer pink around the bone. In the last 20 minutes, turn on broiler to brown chicken (about 10 minutes on each side). Use middle rack of oven to keep chicken from burning. Check frequently.

Serve chicken and gravy over rice.

Serves 6–8.

LEMON CHICKEN

Sweet and tart. This is a great dish for lemon lovers.

2 boned chicken breasts, skinned and cut in half lengthwise

canola oil, for deep frying

1 medium zucchini, cut lengthwise into quarters

8 large mushrooms, whole

MARINADE

1 tablespoon canola oil

1 egg, beaten

2 teaspoons cornstarch

1 teaspoon low-sodium soy sauce

¼ teaspoon fresh ground black pepper

BATTER

1 cup flour

¼ cup cornstarch

1½ teaspoons baking powder

1 tablespoon canola oil

1 cup ice water

LEMON SAUCE

1 tablespoon canola oil

1 large lemon, cut in half lengthwise and thinly sliced

1 cup chicken soup stock or 1 cup water plus 1 teaspoon pareve chicken soup mix, prepared according to package directions

3 tablespoons fresh lemon juice

7 tablespoons sugar

1 tablespoon cornstarch, plus 1 tablespoon water, for thickening

Mix ingredients for marinade together. Coat chicken evenly with mixture and chill for 30 minutes.

To prepare batter, combine flour, cornstarch, and baking powder. Mix well. Stir in oil and ice water. Refrigerate 30 minutes.

Heat oil for lemon sauce in a small saucepan over low heat. Add sliced lemons and sauté for 40 seconds. Add chicken soup stock, lemon juice, and sugar. Simmer for 2 minutes. Mix together cornstarch and water and add slowly to lemon sauce, stirring constantly until thickened. Remove from heat and set aside.

Coat marinated chicken evenly with batter. Fry chicken in 1½-inch-deep oil over medium-low heat. Do not overcrowd pan. If it appears that the chicken is browning before the inside is cooked, reduce heat. Cook until golden brown on outside and fully cooked inside (5–7 minutes).

Use remaining batter to coat zucchini and mushrooms. Deep-fry in oil.

Slice chicken crosswise into 1-inch pieces and serve with zucchini, mushrooms, and white rice. Reheat sauce and pour over sliced chicken.

Serves 6.

MU SHU CHICKEN M

*This is the dish that made me fall in love with Chinese food as a child.
Try it on your kids and see if they have the same reaction.*

2 chicken breasts, cut
lengthwise into ½-inch strips

8 spring roll wrappers, or 6
tortillas

¼ cup hoisin sauce

MARINADE

1 tablespoon cornstarch

1 tablespoon water

1 teaspoon low-sodium soy
sauce

FILLING

3 eggs, beaten

4–5 tablespoons canola oil

8 cups shredded cabbage and
carrot mix

4 green onions, sliced

1 tablespoon pareve chicken
soup mix

1 teaspoon sugar

1 teaspoon low-sodium soy sauce

1 cup bean sprouts

Mix together marinade ingredients and coat chicken. Set aside. In a frying pan, scramble eggs in 1 tablespoon oil over medium heat. Remove eggs to a separate plate. Heat 2 tablespoons oil in pan. Add chicken and stir-fry over medium heat for 2–3 minutes. Remove from pan. Add 1–2 tablespoons oil to pan. Add cabbage and carrot mix. Fry until cabbage becomes translucent but still somewhat crisp. Add green onions, chicken soup mix, sugar, soy sauce, stir-fried chicken, eggs, and bean sprouts. Heat for about 1 minute.

Heat spring roll wrappers a few at a time, for approximately 20 seconds in a microwave. Lay a wrapper on a dry surface. Put ¼ cup of chicken-vegetable mixture across lower side of wrapper. Top with approximately 1 teaspoon hoisin sauce. Fold sides one over the other and tuck the bottom up so the filling won't fall out, or wrap like a burrito.

Serve and eat by hand.

Serves 3–4.

Variation: Substitute tofu for chicken. Cut 1 block of tofu into matchsticks, and lightly brown in 1–2 tablespoons canola oil over medium-high heat. Follow directions above.

BEEF WITH BROCCOLI

The fresh ginger makes this dish spectacular.

1 pound tender beef, cut across grain into 2-inch strips

1–2 pounds fresh broccoli

3 tablespoons canola oil

2 tablespoons plus one teaspoon fresh ginger, chopped

3 green onions, cut into 2-inch pieces, sliced on diagonal

1 tablespoon plus 1 teaspoon cornstarch plus 2 tablespoons water, for thickening

MARINADE

2 teaspoons sugar

1 tablespoon low-sodium soy sauce

1 tablespoon plus one teaspoon cornstarch

2 tablespoons cold water

SAUCE

3 tablespoons low-sodium soy sauce

1 tablespoon blackstrap molasses

1 tablespoon dry red wine

2 teaspoons sugar

½ cup water plus ½ teaspoon pareve chicken soup mix, prepared according to package directions

Mix together marinade ingredients and marinate meat for 30 minutes. Combine ingredients for sauce and set aside. Boil water in a pot, and immerse broccoli for 30 seconds. Rinse under cold water and place in a separate bowl. Heat 2 tablespoons oil in a frying pan and add marinated meat. Stir-fry for 5–6 minutes, or until meat is browned. Remove meat to a separate bowl. Add 1 tablespoon oil, ginger, and green onions to frying pan and stir-fry for 30 seconds to 1 minute. Add sauce. Bring to a boil. Mix cornstarch and water and add to sauce, stirring constantly. Return meat and broccoli to pan and heat thoroughly.

Serves 4–6.

BEEF CHOW FUN ▧

A favorite in our family. The rice noodles make this dish a special treat.

1 pound tender beef, cut into
    2 x ¼ inch slices

3 tablespoons canola oil

1 large onion, sliced lengthwise

4 cloves garlic, slivered

4 large green onions, cut into
    2-inch pieces

1 14-ounce package wide rice
    noodles, soaked in warm
    water for 30 minutes or until
    soft, and drained

½ cup water plus ½ teaspoon
    pareve chicken soup mix,
    prepared according to package
    directions

5 tablespoons low-sodium soy sauce

4 cups bean sprouts

¼ teaspoon crushed red pepper
    flakes, optional

MARINADE

1 tablespoon low-sodium soy sauce

2 teaspoons cornstarch

1 tablespoon water

Mix together marinade ingredients and marinate sliced beef for ½ hour. In a frying pan, heat 1 tablespoon oil over medium heat. Add onions. Fry for 1 minute. Add marinated meat and stir-fry 3–5 minutes. Add garlic and green onions and stir-fry for an additional minute. Remove beef, onion, and garlic to a bowl. Heat 2 tablespoons of oil in pan on medium-high heat and add noodles. Stir-fry for 3–4 minutes. Add pareve chicken soup and soy sauce to the noodles. Return beef and onions back to the pan and reheat. Stir in bean sprouts 1 minute before serving. Sprinkle with crushed red pepper flakes.

Serves 6–8.

CHINESE

MONGOLIAN BEEF

The combination of green and white onions make this dish a winner.

1 pound beef, cut into 2 x ¼ inch slices

3 tablespoons canola oil

1 large onion, sliced lengthwise

5 cloves garlic, slivered

4 large green onions, cut into 2-inch pieces

¼ teaspoon crushed red pepper flakes, optional

MARINADE

1 tablespoon low-sodium soy sauce

2 teaspoons cornstarch

1 tablespoon water

SAUCE

1 cup water plus 1 teaspoon pareve chicken soup mix, prepared according to package directions

1 tablespoon low-sodium soy sauce

1 tablespoon cornstarch

Mix together marinade ingredients and marinate beef for 15 minutes. Combine ingredients for sauce and set aside. Heat a pan on medium-high heat. Add 1 tablespoon oil to pan. Add onion and fry for 1 minute. Add 1 more tablespoon oil and marinated meat. Stir-fry until meat is no longer pink. Add garlic and green onions and continue to stir-fry until green onions are slightly limp. Add crushed red pepper flakes. Add sauce, and stir until gravy thickens.

Serve over white rice.

Serves 6–8.

BEEF WITH BEAN SPROUTS

One of the first Chinese dishes I was introduced to. This simple delicacy has remained close to my heart.

3 tablespoons canola oil

1 pound tender beef, cut into 3 x ¼ inch strips

3 tablespoons low-sodium soy sauce

6 cloves garlic, minced

¼ pound mushrooms, sliced

1 cup water plus 1 teaspoon pareve chicken soup mix, prepared according to package directions

2 tablespoons cornstarch plus 3 tablespoons water, for thickening

3 green onions, cut into 3-inch pieces

2 8-ounce packages bean sprouts (approximately 4 cups)

Heat frying pan over medium-high heat and add oil. Add meat and stir-fry until medium-well done. Add soy sauce, garlic, and mushrooms and stir-fry until mushrooms are browned. Add pareve chicken soup. Bring to a boil. Mix together cornstarch and water and stir into pan until gravy thickens. Add green onions and cook for 1 minute. Add bean sprouts. Heat thoroughly immediately before serving.

Serves 4–6.

PEPPER STEAK M

A classic dish made simple.

3 tablespoons canola oil

1 pound steak, cut into
    2 x ½ inch strips

2 green peppers, cut into 2-inch
    strips

2 red peppers, cut into 2-inch
    strips

1–2 medium onions, cut into
    2-inch cubes

2 large cloves garlic, sliced

2 tablespoons cornstarch plus
    2 tablespoons water, for
    thickening

MARINADE

1 tablespoon canola oil

1 teaspoon cornstarch

1 teaspoon low-sodium soy sauce

SAUCE

1 cup chicken soup stock, or 1
    cup water plus 1 teapoon
    pareve chicken soup mix,
prepared according to package
    directions

⅛ teaspoon fresh ground black
    pepper

1 teaspoon sugar

2 tablespoons low-sodium soy
    sauce

Combine marinade ingredients and
marinate meat 15–20 minutes. In a
separate bowl, mix together ingredients for sauce and set aside. Heat
frying pan over medium-high heat
and add oil to pan. Add marinated
meat and stir-fry until browned.
Add peppers, onions, and garlic.
Cook another 2 minutes. Add
sauce mixture and bring to a boil.
Combine cornstarch with water and
add to pan, stirring constantly until
thickened. Taste to make sure all
cornstarch taste is gone.

Serve hot over white rice.

Serves 4–6.

GARLIC FISH WITH VEGETABLES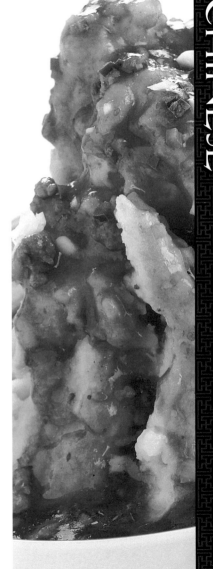

Great for dinner during the Nine Days.

4 white fish fillets (tilapia or cod), cut into 2 x 2 inch pieces

5 tablespoons cornstarch

canola oil, for frying

MARINADE

1 teaspoon sesame oil

1 tablespoon cornstarch

2 tablespoons low-sodium soy sauce

1 tablespoon canola oil

pinch of salt

SAUCE

1 tablespoon canola oil

10 cloves garlic, coarsely chopped

1 cup water plus 1 teaspoon pareve chicken soup mix, prepared according to package directions

1 tablespoon low-sodium soy sauce

1–2 teaspoons sugar

1 tablespoon cornstarch plus 1 tablespoon water, for thickening

STIR-FRIED VEGETABLES

2–3 tablespoons canola oil

4 carrots, julienned

3 medium zucchini, sliced into half-circles

1 onion, sliced lengthwise into thin strips

½–1 jalapeño pepper, diced, optional

4 green onions, cut diagonally into 2-inch pieces

Mix marinade ingredients together. Marinate fish 20–30 minutes. To prepare sauce, heat oil in a pan. Add garlic and fry 1–2 minutes. Lower heat and add pareve chicken soup, soy sauce, and sugar. Stir. Raise heat to medium. Bring sauce to a boil. Mix together cornstarch and water and add to sauce, stirring

constantly to thicken. Remove from heat and set aside.

To prepare vegetables, heat oil in a frying pan over medium-high heat. Add carrots, zucchini, onion, and jalapeño pepper and stir-fry until cooked but still crisp. Add green onions and cook 1 more minute. Remove vegetables to a separate bowl.

To fry fish, cover the bottom of a large frying pan with oil ½-inch deep and heat over medium-high heat. Coat each piece of fish with cornstarch. Fry fish in oil 5–10 minutes, until it is cooked through. When fish is golden brown, remove to a platter covered with paper towels to drain excess oil.

To serve: Prepare a platter of white rice. Top with vegetables and then fish. Pour sauce over the entire dish for an elegant presentation.

Serves 4–6.

CHINESE FISH WITH SESAME SAUCE □

The sesame oil really brings this sauce to life.

4 white fish fillets (tilapia or sole), cut into 2-inch pieces

5–6 tablespoons cornstarch

2 eggs

canola oil, for frying

1 tablespoon sesame seeds, for garnish

MARINADE

2 tablespoons low-sodium soy sauce

1 teaspoon sesame oil

2 cloves garlic, finely chopped

⅛ teaspoon crushed red pepper flakes, optional

SAUCE

1 cup water plus 1 teaspoon pareve chicken soup mix, prepared according to package directions

1 tablespoon low-sodium soy sauce

1 tablespoon sesame oil

⅛ teaspoon crushed red pepper flakes

1 tablespoon cornstarch plus 1 tablespoon water, for thickening

Mix together marinade ingredients and marinate fish 10–15 minutes. In a separate pan, prepare sauce. Combine pareve chicken soup, soy sauce, sesame oil, and crushed red pepper flakes and bring to a boil. Lower heat. In a separate bowl, mix together cornstarch and water, and add to sauce, stirring constantly for 3–4 minutes. Remove from heat and set aside.

Prepare 5–6 tablespoons cornstarch in a bowl. In a separate bowl, beat 2 eggs. Cover bottom of a pan with oil and heat. Coat each fish fillet with cornstarch, then egg. Fry until golden brown on both sides, 5–10 minutes. Reheat sauce. To serve, prepare a platter of white rice. Place fish pieces on top and pour sauce over the fish. Sprinkle with sesame seeds.

Serves 4.

GINGER BAKED FISH WITH GREEN ONIONS □

A deliciously healthy choice. This dish is essentially fat-free.

6 fish fillets (tilapia, cod, or salmon)

1 tablespoon garlic, finely chopped

1 tablespoon fresh ginger, finely chopped

6 tablespoons low-sodium soy sauce

3 large green onions, cut diagonally into 1-inch pieces

Place fish fillets in a baking pan. Sprinkle with garlic and ginger. Pour 1 tablespoon soy sauce on each fillet. Cover fish with green onions and bake for 20–30 minutes, depending on thickness of fish.

Serve with white rice.

Serves 6.

TOFU WITH STIR-FRIED BOK CHOY  M/D

The sauce in this dish makes it a one-of-a-kind tofu treat.

2 16-ounce blocks tofu, cut into 2-inch squares

3–4 tablespoons canola oil

1 medium onion, diced

6–8 cups bok choy, baby bok choy, or beet greens, chopped

3 large green onions, cut into 2-inch pieces

5 large cloves garlic, sliced into ¼-inch chunks

1 cup chicken soup stock, or 1 cup water plus 1 teaspoon pareve chicken soup mix, prepared according to package directions

2 tablespoons low-sodium soy sauce

2 tablespoons blackstrap molasses

1 tablespoon cornstarch plus 1 tablespoon water, for thickening

Fry tofu in 2 batches in 2 tablespoons of oil, until golden brown. Remove from pan and drain on a paper towel. Add 1–2 tablespoons oil and fry onion, bok choy, green onions, and garlic. Stir-fry over a medium heat for 2 minutes. Combine vegetables and tofu in a bowl. Add chicken soup stock to frying pan. Bring to a boil. Stir in soy sauce and molasses. Mix together cornstarch and water and add to pan, stirring constantly until thickened. Return tofu and bok choy to frying pan and reheat.

Serve over rice.

Serves 8.

CHINESE

37

MA-PO TOFU Ⓟ

*This is my absolute favorite tofu dish.
It can be prepared in minutes and it is delicious.*

5 tablespoons canola oil

2 16-ounce blocks tofu, diced into
½-inch cubes and drained

1 heaping cup fresh
mushrooms, diced

3 tablespoons minced garlic

2 cups water plus 2 teaspoons
pareve chicken soup mix,
prepared according to package
directions

1 teaspoon crushed red pepper
flakes, optional

4 tablespoons low-sodium soy
sauce

1 tablespoon sesame oil

2 tablespoons cornstarch plus
2 tablespoons water, for
thickening

2 green onions, thinly sliced

Heat a large frying pan over high
heat and add 4 tablespoons oil.
Add tofu and sauté until lightly
browned. Remove tofu from pan
and set aside. Add mushrooms
and garlic to pan and sauté 2
minutes. Add pareve chicken
soup, crushed red pepper flakes,
and soy sauce. Return tofu to
pan. Cook 3–5 minutes. Mix
cornstarch with water and add to
tofu mixture. Stir constantly until
thickened. Add green onions and
sesame oil. Stir and serve. Add additional crushed red pepper flakes
if you like things really spicy. Be
careful! A little goes a long way.

Serves 6–8.

SZECHUAN EGGPLANT

This is a favorite at our Shabbos table. Everyone who tries it asks for the recipe.

3 medium eggplants, unpeeled, cut into 1-inch cubes

canola oil, for frying

6 tablespoons garlic, chopped

green onions, chopped, for garnish

SAUCE

4 tablespoons low-sodium soy sauce

5 tablespoons sugar

1 cup water plus 1 teaspoon pareve chicken soup mix, prepared according to package directions

2 tablespoons plus 1 teaspoon white vinegar

1 teaspoon crushed red pepper flakes

Soak eggplant in salt water for 15–30 minutes. Rinse and drain well. Pour oil to cover bottom of a large frying pan ¼ inch deep. Place half of eggplant cubes in pan. Fry over high heat until soft, 5–8 minutes. Add more oil if necessary. Remove eggplant from pan and set aside. Repeat with second batch of eggplant. When soft, remove from pan. Add 1 teaspoon oil and chopped garlic to pan and fry for a few seconds over low heat. Combine sauce ingredients. Add to pan and bring to a boil. Return eggplant to pan and cook for 5 minutes.

Serve topped with chopped green onions.

Serves 10.

GREEN BEANS WITH GARLIC

A delicious way to prepare green beans. Great for garlic lovers.

3 tablespoons canola oil

1 pound fresh or frozen green beans

5 cloves garlic, chopped

1 tablespoon low-sodium soy sauce, optional

In a large frying pan, heat oil over medium heat. Add green beans and stir-fry until tender but still bright green, approximately 5–7 minutes. Be careful not to overcook. Add garlic and fry for another 1–2 minutes. Add a splash of soy sauce or serve as is.

Serves 4–6.

SPICY STIR-FRIED VEGETABLES ⬠

Easy and nutritious. Use whatever veggies you have on hand.

2 tablespoons canola oil

1 onion, cut into chunks

4 carrots, sliced diagonally, or
    1 cup baby carrots

2 small zucchini, sliced into
    ½-inch slices, optional

1 cup broccoli florets

5 cloves garlic, slivered

2–4 tablespoons low-sodium
    soy sauce

½ teaspoon crushed red pepper
    flakes

1–2 teaspoons sugar

1 cup snow peas, optional

¼ cup slivered almonds,
    optional

Heat oil in pan over medium heat. Add onion and stir-fry until lightly browned, 1–2 minutes. Remove onion and set aside. Reheat pan and add more oil if necessary. Add carrots. Stir-fry until cooked but still crisp, 5–7 minutes. Add zucchini and broccoli, and continue to stir-fry for another 2 minutes. Return onions to pan to reheat. Add garlic and continue to stir-fry an additional 30 seconds. Add soy sauce, crushed red pepper flakes, and sugar. Add snow peas and cook 1 more minute.

Serve over white rice. Top with almonds if desired.

Serves 6–8.

EGG FOO YONG

A delicious vegetarian main dish.

5 tablespoons canola oil

1 medium onion, chopped

2 cups fresh mushrooms, sliced into ½-inch slices

6 eggs, beaten

1 tablespoon low-sodium soy sauce

¼ cup flour

1 8-ounce package bean sprouts (2 cups)

2 green onions, chopped into ¼-inch pieces

GRAVY

2 cups water plus 2 teaspoons pareve chicken soup mix, prepared according to package directions

1 tablespoon low-sodium soy sauce

2 tablespoons cornstarch plus

2 tablespoons water, for thickening

Heat a large frying pan over medium-high heat. Add 2 tablespoons oil. Add onion and mushrooms and stir-fry until onions are slightly translucent. Set aside. In a separate bowl, mix eggs, soy sauce, flour, bean sprouts, and green onions. Add half of onion and mushroom mix. Mix well. Heat 2 tablespoons oil in a frying pan. Heat over medium-high heat. Pour ½ cup of egg mixture into pan to form a patty. Continue forming patties with entire mixture, adding oil as necessary. When egg runs, fold it back into patty. Flatten with a spatula. Patties will look like small omelets. Cook 2–3 minutes on each side or until brown on both sides and eggs are no longer runny.

Remove from pan and drain on paper towels. Cover lightly with an aluminum foil tent to keep warm until you're finished frying all the patties.

To prepare gravy, heat pareve chicken soup in a saucepan. Add soy sauce and the rest of the sautéed onions and mushrooms. Bring to a boil over a medium-high heat. Mix together cornstarch and water and add to pan, stirring constantly for smooth consistency. Reduce heat to medium and continue to stir for 1–2 minutes or until mixture thickens and doesn't taste like cornstarch.

Serve gravy over egg foo yong patties and white rice.

Serves 6–8.

FRIED RICE

A great way to turn leftover rice into something special.

5 tablespoons canola oil

6 eggs, beaten lightly

6 cups cooked rice

4–5 tablespoons low-sodium soy sauce, or to taste

1 cup frozen peas and carrots

3 green onions, thinly sliced

Heat 1 tablespoon oil in a large frying pan over medium heat.

Scramble eggs and remove to a separate bowl. Pour 4 tablespoons oil and cooked rice into pan. Stir until rice is lightly coated with oil. Stir in soy sauce. Add scrambled eggs, peas and carrots, and green onion. Stir and cook until heated through. Add more soy sauce according to taste.

Serves 4–6.

WHITE RICE

For most Asian meals.

4 cups water

2 cups uncooked white rice

Bring water to a boil. Add rice and stir. Bring back to a boil and stir. Reduce heat and cover. Simmer for 20 minutes without stirring or lifting the lid. This should make perfect rice every time.

Serves 6.

CHOW MEIN D

Noodles are fun for all ages, but kids especially love them.

3 tablespoons canola oil

1 medium onion, sliced lengthwise and cut in half

3–4 cups shredded cabbage and carrot mix

1 16-ounce package spaghetti or capellini noodles, cooked al dente, drained, and rinsed in cold water

1 teaspoon garlic powder

6 tablespoons low-sodium soy sauce

1 tablespoon sesame oil

2 green onions, cut into 2-inch pieces

2 cups bean sprouts, optional

½ teaspoon salt, optional

Heat a large frying pan over medium-high heat. Add 1 tablespoon canola oil, and sauté onion until translucent. Add another tablespoon canola oil and heat. Add cabbage and carrot mix and stir-fry until cabbage is almost translucent. Remove to a separate bowl. Heat remaining tablespoon canola oil in pan and add noodles, coating thoroughly with oil. In a separate bowl, mix garlic powder, soy sauce, and sesame oil, and add to pan. Add sautéed vegetables, green onions, and bean sprouts. Add salt to taste. Stir, heat thoroughly, and serve.

Serves 6.

PEANUT BUTTER NOODLES D

I've never forgotten my first Sukkos in Israel. My aunt served these noodles, and they've been a favorite ever since.

1 16-ounce package spaghetti, cooked al dente, drained, and rinsed with cold water

SAUCE

½ cup creamy peanut butter

4 tablespoons low-sodium soy sauce

3 teaspoons sesame oil

½ cup plus 3 tablespoons water

⅛ teaspoon salt, optional

4 green onions, finely chopped

Combine peanut butter, soy sauce, sesame oil, salt, and water, and mix until reaching a smooth consistency. Pour sauce over spaghetti immediately before serving and mix well. You may need to add a little extra water after you pour the sauce over the noodles to reach a smooth consistency. If so, add 1 tablespoon at a time until reaching desired consistency. Top with chopped green onions.

Serve at room temperature.

Serves 6–8.

Note: Leftover sauce will thicken. Add a small amount of water to regain smooth consistency.

COLD SESAME NOODLE SALAD 🄿

Great for Shabbos lunch.
These noodles are even better after sitting in the fridge overnight.

1 16-ounce package spaghetti
or capellini noodles, cooked,
drained, and rinsed under
cold water

DRESSING

¼ cup canola oil

1 tablespoon sesame oil

¼ cup sugar

½ teaspoon crushed red pepper
flakes

½ cup sliced green onions

2 tablespoons toasted sesame
seeds (see page 21)

¼ cup plus 1 tablespoon low-
sodium soy sauce

In a bowl, combine all ingredients for dressing. Mix well. Pour
dressing over cooked noodles and
stir thoroughly. Let chill for at
least 30 minutes or serve at room
temperature.

Serves 6–8 as a side dish.

SHANGHAI-STYLE CHOW MEIN ⬢

This dish is worth the effort. It is absolutely amazing.

canola oil, for frying

½ cup raw almonds with skins

6 stalks celery, chopped into ½-inch pieces

1–2 bunches bok choy or beet greens, white stems removed, cut into ½-inch pieces, leaves shredded into 1-inch pieces

2 green onions, cut into ¼-inch pieces

6 cloves garlic, slivered

1 16-ounce package thin spaghetti or capellini noodles, cooked and drained

pan-toasted almonds, for garnish

GRAVY

2 cups water plus 2 teaspoons pareve chicken soup mix, prepared according to package directions

2–3 tablespoons low-sodium soy sauce, or to taste

3 tablespoons cornstarch plus 3 tablespoons water, for thickening

Heat 1 tablespoon oil over medium heat. Add almonds and stir-fry until they start to brown. Remove to a plate and set aside. Add 1 tablespoon oil to pan and sauté celery and bok choy. Remove to a large bowl when still crisp. Place green onions and garlic in pan and sauté 1 minute. Add to bowl of stir-fried vegetables.

Add 3–4 tablespoons oil to pan. Add half of noodles and heat on medium-high without stirring Flatten to form a large pancake. Cook 3–4 minutes or until bottom of pancake is brown and golden. Using a large spatula or a plate larger than your pan, carefully flip noodle pancake over. Add more oil to pan if needed. Continue to cook on the other side until nicely browned. Remove from frying pan and keep warm in oven while preparing second noodle pancake.

Reheat pan on high and return sautéed vegetables to pan. In a separate pot, combine pareve chicken soup with soy sauce for gravy and bring to a boil. Mix together cornstarch and water and add to gravy, stirring constantly over medium heat. Cook for 1–2 minutes and taste to make sure there is no cornstarch taste. If there is, cook 1 minute longer.

Cut noodles into pie-shaped wedges and spoon vegetable mixture on top. Top with pan-toasted almonds.

Serves 4–6.

Variation: This recipe lends itself to additional ingredients such as toasted walnuts, mushrooms, onions, carrots, chicken, beef, tofu, sesame oil, and fresh ginger. Stir-fry and add to vegetables.

ALMOND COOKIES

These cookies are easy to make and come out great every time. Make them with your kids and let them stick the almonds in the middle.

2¼ cups flour

1½ teaspoons baking powder

¾ cup sugar

1 cup margarine

1 egg

2 teaspoons almond extract

1 handful blanched almonds

1 egg, beaten, for glaze

Mix dry ingredients in a bowl. In a separate bowl, mix together margarine, egg, and almond extract. Combine wet and dry ingredients and mix well. Roll dough into balls about 1½ inches wide. Place on a cookie sheet, leaving 2 inches between each ball. Press 1 almond into the center of each cookie. Do not flatten cookie. Brush beaten egg onto cookies and bake in a preheated 350° oven for 10–20 minutes, depending on how crunchy you like them.

Yields 2 dozen cookies.

ASIAN FRUIT SALAD

A light and sweet ending to a wonderful Chinese dinner.

2 cans mandarin oranges, drained

1 20-ounce can lychee, liquid reserved

2 cups grapes

In a large bowl, combine mandarin oranges, lychee fruit with syrup, and grapes.

Serves 6–8.

Note: You can also serve sorbet or quartered oranges as dessert after a Chinese meal.

■ B E V E R A G E S ■

JASMINE OR OOLONG TEA

The perfect ending to a Chinese meal.

2 jasmine or oolong tea bags

4 cups hot water

Prepare tea according to package directions. Steep until ready. Serve hot.

Serves 4–6.

JAPANESE

SUSHI WITH FISH AND VEGETABLES ⬛

We like to serve sushi on Shabbos as an elegant fish course. Our guests are always amazed when we bring out a giant platter on Friday night. The cost is minimal and the pleasure is fit for a Shabbos feast.

8 nori sheets (dried seaweed)

¼ pound sushi-grade fish (salmon, lox, sea bass, tuna, or yellowtail), cut against grain into 2 x ¼ inch pieces, or ¼ pound tofu, cut into ¼-inch strips

1 tablespoon canola oil, if using tofu

VEGETABLES

2 carrots, julienned

1 cucumber, cut into thin 2-inch strips

3 green onions, cut into thin 2-inch strips

1 avocado, cut into thin 2-inch strips, optional

6 cups cooked sushi rice (see page 49), cooled

Fry tofu in oil until lightly brown. Pat ¾ cup sushi rice onto 1 sheet nori, covering bottom ⅔ of nori. Leave top ⅓ plain. Lay a row of fish or tofu, and vegetables of your choice across bottom of nori, on top of rice. (Keep a bowl of water next to you while rolling the sushi to moisten your hands, since this will make the preparation easier.) Roll tightly from bottom. Wait a moment to let nori moisten and form a seal. Continue with remaining ingredients.

Slice each sushi roll into 8 pieces. Arrange on a serving platter. See page 49 for serving instructions.

Serves 8–16.

SUSHI RICE

This sweet vinegared rice gives sushi its unique flavor.

3¾ cups water

2 cups uncooked sushi rice

3 tablespoons rice vinegar

3 tablespoons plus 2 teaspoons sugar

Bring water to a boil. Add rice, vinegar, and sugar. Stir thoroughly, cover, and reduce heat to simmer for 20 minutes. When rice is fully cooked, turn off heat and let cool uncovered.

Makes rice for 7–8 sushi rolls.

ENGLISH MUSTARD DIPPING SAUCE

Great if you are on a low-sodium diet. Use this delicious mayo dip instead of soy sauce with your sushi.

1 tablespoon dry English mustard

½ cup mayonnaise

Mix mustard and mayonnaise together and stir until smooth.

Serves 6–8.

SOY SAUCE AND WASABI

Soy sauce and wasabi are classic accompaniments to sushi.

½ cup low-sodium soy sauce

2 tablespoons wasabi powder, prepared according to package directions

Set a small dish for soy sauce and wasabi in front of each person. Serve wasabi in a small mound on sushi tray. Each person can pour soy sauce into their dish and add a little wasabi and stir it into the soy sauce. Wasabi is spicy; test it to see how much you like.

WASABI DIPPING SAUCE

An unusual twist on classic wasabi.

1 tablespoon wasabi powder

½ cup mayonnaise

Mix wasabi and mayonnaise together and stir until smooth.

Serves 6–8.

49

FISH AND VEGETABLE TEMPURA

Great before a fast. Fried food keeps you full longer.

2 zucchini, sliced into ½-inch slices

2 onions, sliced into ½-inch rings

2 carrots, sliced diagonally into ¼-inch pieces

2 small eggplants, sliced into ½-inch slices

½ pound medium-sized mushrooms

1 pound boneless fish (cod or salmon), cut into 2 x 2 inch cubes

canola oil, for deep-frying

BATTER

1 cup ice water

1 egg

1 cup flour

Mix together batter ingredients. Heat oil in a large frying pan over high heat and check if oil is hot enough by dropping a small amount of batter into it. If the batter rises, oil is ready. Coat vegetables in batter and place into the hot oil piece by piece. Be careful not to crowd pan. Watch the tempura carefully and flip over when light golden brown. Once they are golden brown on both sides, remove to a platter covered with paper towels or to an aluminum pan and keep warm in a 200° oven until all the vegetables are fried. Fry fish last, for approximately 3–5 minutes, following the same procedure. Check that fish is cooked through.

Serves 6–8 as an appetizer, or 4–6 as a main dish.

TEMPURA DIPPING SAUCE

This sauce is sweet, light, and delicious.

¼ cup low-sodium soy sauce

¼ cup mirin (sweet seasoning sauce)

¼ cup water

1 tablespoon sugar

Mix all ingredients together. Heat in a medium-size pan over medium heat until sugar is dissolved. Adjust seasoning if necessary. Let cool and serve.

Serves 6–8.

ASIAN RED CABBAGE SALAD ▫

The dressing on this salad is fantastic.

cups shredded red cabbage

ablespoon each black and
  white sesame seeds

up bean sprouts

reen onions, sliced

arrots, thinly sliced

nushrooms, sliced

cup cilantro, optional

SSING

cup canola oil

cup rice vinegar

ablespoon low-sodium soy
  sauce

ablespoon sugar, optional

ablespoon toasted sesame
  seeds (see page 21)

easpoon sesame oil

Combine vegetables in a salad
bowl. In a separate bowl, combine dressing ingredients. Add
dressing to salad and mix well.
Let stand 10–15 minutes before
serving.

Serves 6–8.

CLASSIC MISO SOUP

This is a simple and delicious soup.
The Japanese also use miso soup to soothe an upset stomach.

8 cups water

miso soup paste, enough for 8 cups water

8 ounces firm tofu, cubed

3 fresh mushrooms, sliced

3 green onions, diced, plus a few more, for garnish

Bring water to a boil in a medium-size saucepan. Add miso paste and stir until the paste is fully dissolved. Add tofu, mushrooms, and green onions. Let simmer 3–5 minutes. Serve with a sprinkle of green onions.

Serves 8.

CHICKEN YAKITORI

Quick and delicious.

2 pounds chicken breasts, cubed or cut into strips

10–15 bamboo skewers, soaked in water for 30 minutes

MARINADE

6 tablespoons sherry

¾ cup low-sodium soy sauce

3 tablespoons mirin (sweet seasoning sauce)

2 teaspoons dark molasses

2 tablespoons sugar

Combine marinade ingredients in a bowl. Add chicken pieces and marinate for 15 minutes. Skewer chicken pieces and place on a hot grill. Cook 3–5 minutes on each side, brushing with marinade every few minutes. Check to make sure the meat is cooked through and remove from grill. Grill temperatures will vary, so these times are approximate. Be careful not to overcook, as the meat will dry out.

Serves 6–8 as a main dish, or 12 as an appetizer.

BEEF SUKIYAKI

Sukiyaki is a wonderful one-dish meal.

2 tablespoons canola oil

1 pound tender beef or steak, sliced as thin as possible across grain into 2-inch strips

2 tablespoons low-sodium soy sauce

1 onion, sliced lengthwise

1 cup fresh mushrooms, sliced

1 16-ounce package tofu, cut into 1-inch cubes, optional

3 green onions, cut into 2–3-inch pieces

SAUCE

4 cups water plus 4 teaspoons pareve chicken soup mix, prepared according to package directions

4 tablespoons mirin (sweet seasoning sauce)

1–2 tablespoons sugar

1 8.8-ounce package cellophane or mung bean noodles, soaked in warm water for 30 minutes

Mix together ingredients for sauce and set aside. Heat oil in a frying pan over medium-high heat. Add sliced meat, soy sauce, onion and mushrooms. Stir-fry until meat is slightly browned. Add sauce to meat mixture and mix together well. Reduce heat to low and add tofu. Add soaked noodles and heat for 1–2 minutes. Add green onions and serve in soup bowls.

Serves 6.

TERIYAKI SALMON ▢

This makes a delicious fish course for Shabbos or sheva berachos. Very easy and very elegant.

2 pounds salmon fillet, or 4–6 portions

TERIYAKI SAUCE

6 cloves garlic, minced

2 tablespoons fresh ginger, diced

4 teaspoons canola oil

½ cup low-sodium soy sauce

¾ cup water

4 tablespoons sugar

2 tablespoons plus 1 teaspoon cornstarch and equal amounts water, for thickening

1 tablespoon sesame seeds

To prepare sauce: Fry garlic and ginger in oil over medium-high heat until fragrant, 30 seconds to 1 minute. Add soy sauce and water. Reduce heat to medium-low. Slowly stir in sugar until it dissolves. Lower heat if necessary. Combine cornstarch and water and add to sauce, stirring constantly to thicken. Add sesame seeds. Pour sauce over salmon and bake at 350° for 30–45 minutes or until salmon flakes easily. Serve with rice.

Serves 6.

VARIATION: TERIYAKI CHICKEN

Option #1: Slice 3 chicken breasts into strips and stir-fry in 2 tablespoons canola oil until cooked through, approximately 3–5 minutes. Add teriyaki sauce and serve over rice.

Option #2: Bake a whole chicken, or chicken parts, at 375° for 20 minutes. Add sauce and continue baking another 40–50 minutes.

Option #3: Teriyaki chicken drumsticks or chicken wings — prepare like option #2 above and bake for 25 minutes until done. Great finger food for a party.

JAPANESE

SPINACH WITH SESAME SEEDS D

A delicious way to get your family to eat spinach.

12 cups fresh spinach leaves, or 16 ounces frozen spinach, defrosted

3 tablespoons water

2 tablespoons white sesame seeds, plain or toasted, for garnish

SAUCE

1 tablespoon rice wine vinegar

2 tablespoons sugar

2 tablespoons low-sodium soy sauce

2 tablespoons mirin (sweet seasoning sauce)

If using fresh spinach, combine spinach and water in a pot or frying pan. Cover and steam until spinach becomes limp, approximately 3 minutes. Drain and allow spinach to cool. In a separate bowl, mix together sauce ingredients and pour over cooled spinach. Garnish with a sprinkle of sesame seeds.

Serves 4–6.

GREEN TEA D

A natural antioxidant. Green tea can be a wonderful pick-me-up.

2 tea bags green tea

4 cups hot water

Prepare tea with hot water according to package directions. Steep until ready.

Serves 4–6

THAI

THAI FISH CAKES

Great for Shabbos Chanukah or when you really want to impress your guests. This fish cake and sauce combination will make a Shabbos to remember.

1 20-ounce frozen gefilte fish roll
1 cup cilantro, chopped
4 large cloves garlic, minced
3 eggs, beaten
5 tablespoons flour
⅛–¼ teaspoon crushed red pepper flakes
3 green onions, chopped
3 tablespoons canola oil, plus additonal oil for frying

Defrost fish roll and mash into a smooth consistency. In a large bowl, combine all ingredients and mix thoroughly. Shape into patties 2½–3 inches wide. Thin patties cook faster and go further, but you can make them any size you like.

Heat oil in a large frying pan over medium-high heat. Add fish cakes and fry until brown on both sides. Add more oil as needed. Remove to a platter covered with paper towels to drain excess oil.

Serve hot or at room temperature with Fish Cake Dipping Sauce (see page 61).

Serves 10–12 as an appetizer, or 4–6 as a main dish.

THAI SPRING ROLLS

*A welcome variation on Chinese egg rolls,
these spring rolls are in a league of their own.*

5–6 tablespoons canola oil, plus additional oil for deep-frying

4 cups diced mushrooms

3 medium carrots, shredded

8 cloves garlic, diced

1 cup cilantro, stems removed

5 green onions, diced

½ package cellophane or mung bean noodles (about 4 ounces), soaked in warm water for 30 minutes and drained

1 cup raw chicken, diced or cut into thin strips

16 spring roll wrappers

Heat 3 tablespoons of oil in a medium-size frying pan. Add vegetables and stir-fry 2–5 minutes. Drain off liquid and remove from pan. Reduce heat to low and add 1 tablespoon oil and noodles. Stir-fry until soft and translucent, 1–2 minutes. Remove noodles from pan and add to vegetables. Add 1–2 tablespoons oil and chicken to pan and stir-fry until chicken is cooked through, 2–5 minutes. Add chicken to vegetables in bowl and stir. Cool.

Place 1 wrapper on a flat surface. Put 2 tablespoons of filling on bottom ⅓ of wrapper. Fold in right and left sides and tightly roll up from bottom. Repeat with the rest of the wrappers. Spring rolls should be thin, about 1½ inches wide. Heat frying pan with oil 2 inches deep. Test to see if oil is hot enough. Fry spring rolls until brown on both sides. Remove to a plate covered with paper towels.

Serve with Thai Spring Roll Sauce (see page 61).

Yields 16 spring rolls.

GRILLED
BEEF AND CHICKEN SATAY Ⓜ

Great for a party or an appetizer for sheva berachos.

1½ pounds tender beef, cut against grain into ½-inch thick slices

1½ pounds boneless chicken breasts, cut against grain into ½-inch slices

charcoal, for grilling

24 bamboo skewers

MARINADE

½ cup low-sodium soy sauce

4 cloves garlic, minced

4 tablespoons canola oil

1 teaspoon crushed red pepper flakes

⅛ teaspoon ground coriander, optional

1 teaspoon ground cumin

2 teaspoons sugar

Soak bamboo skewers in water for 30 minutes. Light fire in grill. While charcoal is heating, mix marinade ingredients together. Skewer meat or chicken and place in a long pan. Marinate 20–30 minutes, turning every 10 minutes. When coals are hot, grill skewers for 3–4 minutes on each side. Grilling time may vary, so watch skewers closely.

Serves 24 as an appetizer, or 12 as a main dish,

Note: Meats can also be grilled under broiler in the oven.

PEANUT SAUCE FOR SATAY

This peanut sauce adds a wonderful flavor to chicken or beef satay.

2 cloves garlic, minced

2 tablespoons canola oil

¼ cup water

½ cup creamy peanut butter

½ cup light coconut milk

½ teaspoon crushed red pepper flakes, or to taste, optional

1 tablespoon sugar

In a medium bowl, combine all ingredients and mix thoroughly. Serve as a dipping sauce with Grilled Beef and Chicken Satay (see page 60) or Cucumber and Carrot Salad (page 62).

Serves 12–24.

Note: If using unsalted peanut butter, add ¼ teaspoon salt.

FISH CAKE DIPPING SAUCE

Light and tangy, this sauce enhances the flavors of fish cakes and spring rolls.

¾ cup rice vinegar

½ cup sugar

¼–½ teaspoon crushed red pepper flakes

1 tablespoon water

Mix ingredients together and serve with Thai Fish Cakes (see page 58).

Variation: For Thai Spring Roll Sauce, add ½ carrot, shredded.

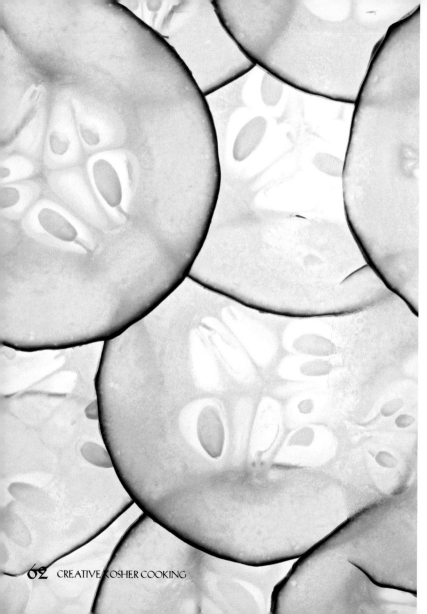

CUCUMBER AND CARROT SALAD ℗

This salad is served as an accompaniment to many Thai dishes. It's particularly delicious with Peanut Sauce (see page 61).

1 cup cucumber rounds (1 medium cucumber)

3 cups bean sprouts

1 cup shredded or julienned carrots

1 green onion, sliced

DRESSING

½ cup sugar

¾ cup rice vinegar or white vinegar

Combine vegetables in a bowl. Dissolve sugar in vinegar for dressing and pour over vegetables. Let sit for a few minutes before serving. If you have time, chill salad so flavors can marry.

Serves 8.

THAI COCONUT CHICKEN SOUP

This soup is so good you'll think you're in a restaurant.

6 cups chicken soup stock

9 mushrooms, sliced

½ teaspoon crushed red pepper flakes, or more if desired

¾ cup raw chicken, diced

2 tablespoons cornstarch

1½ cups low-fat coconut milk

3 cups bean sprouts, plus additonal bean sprouts for garnish, optional

coconut flakes, for garnish, optional

Bring chicken soup stock to a boil. Add mushrooms and crushed red pepper flakes, and cook for 2 minutes. In a separate bowl, coat chicken with cornstarch. Add chicken to pot, stir, and cook for another 2 minutes. Add coconut milk and bean sprouts. Heat to just under a boil, to prevent coconut milk from curdling.

Serve topped with bean spouts and coconut flakes, if desired.

Serves 8.

Note: Some *poskim* recommend adding shredded coconut to a meat dish that contains coconut milk.

THAI BARBECUE CHICKEN

A wonderful grilled treat.

4 whole boneless chicken breasts
   with skin, cut in half, or 8 thighs

charcoal, for grilling

MARINADE

4 tablespoons canola oil

6 tablespoons sugar

6 tablespoons lemon juice

8–12 cloves garlic, minced

1 teaspoon salt

2 tablespoons rice vinegar

1 green chili, seeded and finely
   diced, optional

Combine marinade ingredients in a glass bowl and add chicken. Marinate for 30–45 minutes. Once charcoal is ready, place chicken on grill and cover with an aluminum foil tent. Cook for 10 minutes on each side, turning to assure even cooking. Check to see if chicken is ready. Grilling time will vary depending on heat of grill.

Serve with jasmine rice (see page 66) and dipping sauce (below).

Serves 6–8.

THAI CHICKEN DIPPING SAUCE

Delicately delicious.

4 tablespoons fresh cilantro,
   finely chopped

2 tablespoons sugar

½ teaspoon salt

4 tablespoons water

2 tablespoons freshly squeezed

   lemon juice

green chili, finely chopped, to
   taste

Mix all ingredients together and let sit for 15 minutes before serving.

Serves 4–8.

THAI BASIL CHICKEN WITH PEPPERS Ⓜ

I had this extraordinary dish in a Thai restaurant in Jerusalem when I was a teenager. It took me years, but I have recreated the recipe here.

1 whole boneless chicken breast, cut into 1-inch strips

2 tablespoons cornstarch

2 tablespoons water

4 tablespoons canola oil

1 large onion, sliced lengthwise

2 large green peppers, sliced lengthwise

1 large red pepper, sliced lengthwise

1 small jalapeño pepper, sliced lengthwise

5 cloves garlic, sliced lengthwise

3 cups fresh basil leaves, packed loosely

SAUCE

½ cup water

½ teaspoon pareve chicken soup mix

2 tablespoons sugar

2 tablespoons low-sodium soy sauce

Mix ingredients for sauce together and set aside. Combine cornstarch and water and coat chicken with mixture. Heat frying pan and add 2 tablespoons oil. Add onion, peppers, garlic, and basil. Stir-fry 1–2 minutes. Remove to a separate bowl. Add 2 more tablespoons oil to pan and stir-fry chicken until golden brown on all sides and cooked thoroughly. Add sauce to pan. Return vegetables to pan. Heat and serve over a bed of jasmine rice (see page 66).

Serves 4–6.

GRILLED ZUCCHINI

An easy and delicious way to add a vegetable recipe to your meal.

4 medium zucchini, cut lengthwise

charcoal, for grilling

MARINADE

2 teaspoons canola oil

3 tablespoons freshly squeezed lemon juice

½ teaspoon salt

½ teaspoon cayenne pepper

Combine marinade ingredients in a large container with a lid. Add zucchini and marinate for 15–20 minutes, turning over occasionally. Meanwhile, heat charcoal in grill. Place zucchini on grill over hot charcoal and cover with aluminum foil. Grill, turning over every 5 minutes until zucchini is tender when pricked with a fork, but not too soft. Cooking time varies from 10–30 minutes, depending on how hot your grill gets.

Serves 6–8.

■ RICE & NOODLES ■

JASMINE RICE

A must for Thai and Southeast Asian meals.

4 cups water

2 cups uncooked jasmine rice

Bring water to a boil. Add rice and stir. Bring back to a boil and stir. Reduce heat and cover. Simmer for 20 minutes without stirring or lifting the lid.

Serves 6.

PAD THAI 🄿

A household favorite when a special lunch or dinner is in order.

4 tablespoons canola oil

8 ounces tofu (½ block), cut into 2 x ½ inch strips

4 cloves garlic, diced

2 eggs, beaten

7 ounces wide rice noodles, soaked in warm water for 30 minutes and drained

½ cup water plus ½ teaspoon pareve chicken soup mix

3 green onions, cut into thin 3-inch pieces

1–2 cups bean sprouts

¼ teaspoon crushed red pepper flakes, optional

½ cup salted peanuts, skinned

1–2 lemons, cut into wedges

SAUCE

1 tablespoon white vinegar

2 tablespoons low-sodium soy sauce

⅛ teaspoon crushed red pepper flakes, optional

3 tablespoons sugar

Mix sauce ingredients and set aside. Heat 1 tablespoon oil in frying pan over medium-high heat. Fry tofu for 2 minutes, add garlic, and fry for 20 seconds more. Remove to a separate bowl. Scramble eggs in frying pan and combine with ready-fried tofu in bowl. Heat 3 tablespoons oil over medium-high heat. Add rice noodles and stir to coat. Cook for 2 minutes. Reduce heat to low, add prepared pareve chicken soup and sauce, and mix well. Add tofu, green onions, bean sprouts, and crushed pepper flakes. Heat for 2 minutes. Top with peanuts and lemon wedges. Squeeze lemon onto dish for extra flavor.

Serves 3 as a main dish.

Note: This recipe doesn't do well doubled. It's better to make two batches than to double the recipe.

THAI ICED TEA

A delicious, cooling treat. Great for Shabbos lunches in the summer.

4 cups hot water plus 4 Lipton tea bags

2 cups vanilla-flavored soy milk

¾ cup sugar

crushed ice cubes

Boil water and pour into a heat-resistant pitcher. Add tea bags and brew tea to double strength (twice as long as usual). Add sugar, stirring until dissolved. Add soy milk. Let cool, and serve in glasses over crushed ice.

Serves 8.

Note: May also be served as a hot tea.

THAI ICED COFFEE

The cardamom gives this coffee a unique and special flavor.

4 cups hot water

4 tablespoons instant coffee

½ teaspoon cardamom

¾ cup sugar

4 cups soy milk

crushed ice or ice cubes

Brew 4 cups coffee. Add sugar and cardamom and stir until dissolved. Add soy milk and serve in a glass of crushed ice or ice cubes.

Serves 8–10.

FILIPINO

LUMPIA

Easy to prepare ahead of time. Great to keep in the freezer for when you have unexpected guests. They freeze beautifully.

2 teaspoons canola oil, plus
    additional oil for deep-frying

½ onion, diced

2 pounds lean ground beef

1 teaspoon salt

2 cups frozen peas and carrots

2 packages spring roll wrappers
    (30 wrappers)

Heat 2 teaspoons canola oil in medium-size frying pan over medium heat. Lightly sauté onion, then add ground beef and salt. Cook on medium heat until meat is browned. Remove from heat and drain oil. Add frozen peas and carrots to ground beef and onion mixture. Allow to cool.

Peel 1 spring roll wrapper off paper and set on a large plate. Keep remaining wrappers covered so they don't dry out. Take 1 heaping tablespoon of ground beef mixture and place on lower ⅓ of wrapper. Fold both right and left side of wrapper toward middle like an envelope and tightly roll from bottom to top. Place lumpia face-side-down in a container or on a plate until all lumpias are assembled. Deep-fry in oil.

Yields 20 lumpia.

Note: **Lumpia can be frozen after they are assembled and can be cooked frozen. They are great for a quick snack or a** *melaveh malkah* **treat.**

CHICKEN ADOBO

Possibly the easiest dish I have ever made — and my husband's absolute favorite. This is a great dish for when you don't have a lot of time but still want to make a wonderful meal.

1 whole chicken, cut into eighths

1 cup water

1 cup white vinegar

⅛ teaspoon freshly ground black pepper

5 cloves garlic, slivered

5 bay leaves

¼ cup low-sodium soy sauce

Place all ingredients in a large pot. Bring to a boil. Reduce heat to a simmer, and cook for 30–50 minutes. Check that chicken is cooked thoroughly.

This dish makes its own wonderful gravy. Serve over white or jasmine rice (see page 66).

Serves 6–8.

PAK BET

Filipino beef stew. A great one-dish meal.

1 pound tender beef, sliced into ½-inch strips

6 tablespoons low-sodium soy sauce

2 medium eggplants, diced

6 tablespoons canola oil

1 large onion, chopped

3 small tomatoes, chopped, juice reserved

6 cloves garlic, diced

1 cup water

2–3 cups fresh or frozen green beans or Asian long beans

Marinate meat in 3 tablespoons soy sauce 15–20 minutes. Soak eggplant in a bowl of cold salt water for 20 minutes. Drain well. Heat a frying pan on medium-high heat and add 3 tablespoons of oil. Add drained eggplant pieces being careful of oil splattering. Fry eggplant until brown. Remove to a bowl. Add 2 more tablespoons oil to pan, with the onion and tomatoes. Stir in garlic. Add 3 tablespoons soy sauce and 1 cup water. Set aside.

In a separate pot, heat 1 tablespoon oil and add beef. Stir-fry on medium high until meat is browned. Add vegetable mixture to pot. Stir well. Bring to a boil, then add green beans and cook 3–4 minutes longer.

Serve over white rice.

Serves 6–8.

FILIPINO GREEN BEANS

Between pepper and tomato sauce, this dish is anything but boring old green beans.

1–2 tablespoons canola oil

1 onion, chopped

1 tomato, diced

½ teaspoon salt

⅛ teaspoon black pepper

1 pound fresh green beans or Asian long beans

½ cup water

Heat canola oil in a large frying pan over medium-high heat. Sauté onion, tomato, salt, and pepper until onion is translucent, 3–5 minutes. Add green beans and water. Simmer partially covered until green beans are tender, 6–10 minutes.

Serves 6.

PANCIT

A delicious rice noodle dish.

5 cups shredded cabbage and carrot mix

8 tablespoons canola oil

1 onion, chopped

4 cloves garlic, slivered

¼ cup green onion, chopped

1 10.5-ounce package thin vermicelli rice noodles, soaked in warm water for 30 minutes and drained

8 tablespoons low-sodium soy sauce

¼–½ teaspoon coarsely ground black pepper

½ 7.5-ounce package cellophane or mung beans noodles, soaked in warm water for 30 minutes and drained

Heat 1 tablespoon of oil in a large frying pan over medium-high heat. Add cabbage and carrot mix and saute for 2 minutes, being careful not to overcook. Remove to a separate bowl. Add 1 tablespoon oil to frying pan and stir-fry onion and garlic for 1 minute. Add green onions. Remove from heat and add to cabbage mixture.

Heat 5 tablespoons oil in pan. Add rice noodles and heat until rice noodles are cooked al dente. Taste to see if they are soft enough. Add 5 tablespoons soy sauce and black pepper. Stir thoroughly and remove to a separate bowl. Heat remaining 1 tablespoon oil in pan. Add cellophane noodles and 1 tablespoon soy sauce. Stir-fry until noodles are translucent, 1–2 minutes. Mix vegetables into noodles and adjust soy sauce and black pepper to taste. Garnish with steamed spinach or bok choy, if desired.

Serves 6–8.

Variation: To serve as a main dish, add shreds of stir-fried chicken or tofu.

FILIPINO FRUIT SALAD D/D

The tropical climate of the Philippines lends itself to fruit-based desserts. Top this salad with fresh whipped cream or a pareve alternative.

1 15-ounce can peaches, diced, juice reserved

1 20-ounce can pineapple chunks, drained

1 cup grapes, cut into halves

1 mango, cut into chunks, optional

½ cup kiwi, sliced into wedges, optional

1 cup watermelon, cubed, optional

pareve or dairy whipped cream, for garnish, optional

Combine all fruit together in a bowl. Pour 1 cup peach juice over salad and garnish with a generous serving of whipped cream.

Serves 4–6.

BANANA LUMPIA D

One of the best Filipino dishes I have ever had. This dessert is quick to make and absolutely delicious.

16 spring roll wrappers

4 whole bananas, cut into quarters lengthwise

4 tablespoons sugar

1 teaspoon cinnamon, optional

canola oil, for deep-frying

Combine sugar and cinnamon in a bowl and coat bananas with the mixture. Take 1 spring roll wrapper and place 1 banana strip on bottom ⅓ of wrapper. Fold in left and right side and roll up from bottom.

Deep-fry on each side until golden brown. Drain on paper towels and serve while still warm.

Yields 16 lumpia. Serves 8.

GINGER TEA D

This tea is great for the immune system.

2 ginger tea bags

4 cups hot water

sugar, to taste, optional

Prepare tea with hot water according to package directions. Steep until ready and add sugar if desired

Serves 4–6.

SOUTHEAST ASIAN

INDONESIAN CHICKEN WINGS

This is a personal favorite. The cumin in this dish will make your taste buds sing.

2 pounds chicken wings

½ cup water

MARINADE

½ cup low-sodium soy sauce

1 onion, sliced

¼ cup basil leaves

½ teaspoon ground cumin

2 cloves garlic, minced

2 teaspoons crushed red pepper flakes, optional

Mix together marinade ingredients and let chicken wings marinate for at least ½ an hour. Add water and pour entire contents into a baking dish. Bake at 350° for 30 minutes. Broil for a few minutes to brown top. Watch carefully to be sure it doesn't burn.

Serve over jasmine rice (see page 66).

Serves 4–6.

VIETNAMESE FIVE-SPICE CHICKEN M

Delicate in flavor. This dish almost tastes smoked over a fire.

6–8 chicken thighs

charcoal, for grilling, optional

MARINADE

3 tablespoons canola oil

2 tablespoons sugar

4 tablespoons low-sodium soy sauce

1 teaspoon Chinese five-spice powder

¼ teaspoon crushed red pepper flakes

4 cloves garlic, minced

3½ tablespoons dry sherry

1½ tablespoons fresh ginger, minced

If grilling, start charcoal in a barbecue grill. Otherwise, preheat oven to broil. In a glass container, combine all ingredients for marinade and mix well. Marinate chicken for 30 minutes.

If grilling, place chicken on grill. Grill for 30–45 minutes, turning every 10–15 minutes. Check to make sure chicken is cooked through. If broiling, place chicken in a baking dish. Broil away from heat in lower third of oven for about 45 minutes, turning over every 15 minutes so as not to burn.

Serves 6.

VIETNAMESE CHICKEN AND CELLOPHANE NOODLES M

These cellophane noodles are actually see-through. The texture is wonderful and as they are made from beans and not wheat, they may be acceptable for those on a wheat-free diet.

3 tablespoons canola oil

3 chicken breasts, cut into bite-sized pieces

1 onion, sliced lengthwise

1 tablespoon fresh ginger, minced

6 tablespoons low-sodium soy sauce

½ teaspoon curry powder, optional

freshly ground black pepper, to taste, optional

1 8-ounce package cellophane or mung bean noodles, soaked in warm water for 30 minutes and drained

Heat oil in a frying pan over medium heat. Add chicken, onion, and ginger and stir-fry for 3–4 minutes until chicken begins to brown. Add soy sauce, curry powder, and black pepper, and stir-fry for 2 minutes. Add noodles to pan and cook for another 3 minutes, stirring constantly. Adjust seasoning to taste.

Serves 6.

INDONESIAN YELLOW RICE ⒟

Beautiful to the eye and delicious to the taste buds.

3 cups uncooked long-grain white rice

3 cups canned coconut milk

4½ cups water

3 teaspoons turmeric

3 tablespoons fresh ginger, chopped

1½ teaspoons salt, or to taste

In a saucepan, combine rice, coconut milk, water, turmeric, ginger, and salt. Stir and bring to a boil over medium heat. Reduce heat to a simmer. Cook covered until liquid has been absorbed, about 20 minutes. Fluff rice. Remove with a fork and serve.

Serves 8–12.

MALAYSIAN SESAME-TOPPED VEGETABLES ▣

A mélange of sweet and tangy. These vegetables are delicious and easy to make.

8 large carrots, sliced into
    ½-inch slices

½ cup water

¼ cup canola oil

3 cloves garlic, finely chopped

5 cups mushrooms, quartered

½ cup white vinegar

¼ cup sugar

2 tablespoons low-sodium soy
    sauce

2 tablespoons plain or toasted
    white sesame seeds

In a covered pot, steam carrots in water 1-inch deep for 3 minutes. Drain excess water. In a separate pan, stir-fry garlic in oil on medium-low heat for 2 minutes. Add carrots, mushrooms, vinegar, and sugar to pan. Keep stirring until vegetables are cooked but still crisp. Add soy sauce. Remove to serving bowl and garnish with sesame seeds.

Serves 6–8.

FRIED BANANAS

A great dessert to accompany any Asian meal.

9 slightly firm bananas, sliced diagonally into thick pieces

6 tablespoons margarine

½ teaspoon sesame seeds, for garnish, optional

SAUCE

6 tablespoons margarine

9 tablespoons sugar

Melt 6 tablespoons of margarine in a frying pan over medium heat. Add bananas and fry for 1–2 minutes. Remove bananas to a separate bowl. Add 6 tablespoons margarine to frying pan for sauce and melt over a low heat. Add sugar and stir together over low heat. When syrup has formed, return bananas to pot. Reheat and serve. Garnish with sesame seeds if desired.

Serves 6.

INDIAN

COLD VEGETABLE RAITA D/P

This salad is known to cool the palate.

4 small cucumbers, thinly sliced

3 tomatoes, thinly sliced

1 onion, thinly sliced and cut in half

DRESSING

6 tablespoons nondairy sour cream or plain yogurt

4 tablespoons fresh chopped dill, or 1 tablespoon dried dill

2 tablespoons water

juice of ½ lemon

4 cloves garlic, diced

Combine vegetables in a bowl. Mix together ingredients for dressing and stir into vegetables. If you have time, chill before serving.

Serves 4–6.

GREEN LENTIL SOUP P

This popular soup is warming, filling, and extremely easy to make.

1 cup dry green lentils

8 cups water

2 tablespoons pareve chicken soup mix

1 onion, chopped

5 cloves garlic, minced

¼ teaspoon crushed red pepper flakes

2 teaspoons Indian curry powder

1 teaspoon lemon juice, optional

Combine all ingredients in a soup pot. Bring to a boil, cover, and cook over medium heat 1–1½ hours, or until lentils are tender. Check while cooking and add more water if necessary.

Serves 4–6.

Note: This is a thick soup. Add an extra cup of water if you prefer it thinner.

CHICKEN CURRY

This is one of my oldest and most treasured recipes.

1 tablespoon canola oil

1 large onion, chopped

3–4 cloves garlic, diced

1 whole chicken, cut up

1 medium-large tomato, diced, or
   1 tablespoon tomato paste

1 cup water

1 avocado, cut into wedges, for
   garnish, optional

SPICE MIXTURE

¼ teaspoon powdered ginger

¼ teaspoon turmeric

¼ teaspoon cayenne pepper

¼ teaspoon cinnamon

¼ teaspoon cloves

¼ teaspoon chili powder

1–2 tablespoons curry powder

¼ teaspoon paprika

In a small bowl, mix spice mixture together. Set aside. In a frying pan, heat oil over medium heat. Sauté onion and garlic for 1–2 minutes, until onion is slightly translucent. Remove to a separate bowl. Place chicken in pan and fry 5–10 minutes, until browned on both sides. Add tomato. Add water and return sautéed onion and garlic to pan. Sprinkle spice mixture over both sides of chicken. Cover pan and reduce heat to low. Cook chicken, turning it over and stirring the gravy after 15 minutes. Cook for 30 minutes and then check that chicken is cooked through and no longer pink inside. If gravy is too thin, uncover chicken and cook a few minutes longer.

Serve on a bed of basmati rice with almond and raisin sambals (see pages 86–87). Garnish with avocado, if desired.

Serves 4–6.

INDIAN

CURRIED TOFU AND ZUCCHINI ⓓ

Indian food makes a great dinner choice for the Nine Days.

4 tablespoons canola oil

4 zucchini, quartered lengthwise and thinly sliced

2 onions, diced

2 16-ounce blocks extra firm tofu, cut into cubes

3 cups water

2 tablespoons curry powder

½ teaspoon salt

Heat frying pan over medium heat. Add 2 tablespoons oil. Add zucchini and stir-fry 3 minutes. Add diced onion and continue to fry for 2 minutes. Add tofu. Continue to sauté, stirring frequently. When vegetables begin to brown, add water, curry powder, and salt. Cover and let water cook down until thickened. Add more water if necessary. Stir frequently. Add more curry or salt to taste.

Serve over basmati rice (see page 86).

Serves 4–6.

INDIAN SWEET POTATOES ⓓ

Sweet and delicious.

4 large sweet potatoes, peeled and sliced into ½-inch slices

¼ cup margarine

2 cups orange juice

¼ cup cinnamon

1 cup black raisins

Boil sweet potatoes until almost tender. Drain water. Melt margarine in a large frying pan. Add sweet potatoes, orange juice, and cinnamon. Continue cooking until sweet potatoes are tender. Add raisins and serve with basmati rice (see page 86).

Serves 8.

RED LENTIL DAHL

A great accompaniment to Chicken Curry (page 83).

1 tablespoon canola oil

1 onion, finely chopped

6 cups water

1 tablespoon pareve chicken
   soup mix

2 cups dried red or green lentils

4 cloves garlic, chopped

⅛ teaspoon crushed red pepper
   flakes

½ teaspoon salt

In a 3-quart soup pot, heat oil over medium-high heat. Add onion and cook until translucent, 1–2 minutes. Add water, chicken soup mix, and lentils. Bring to a boil over high heat, covered. Cook for 5 minutes.

Cook covered over medium heat, stirring often. Add water if necessary to prevent the dahl from drying out. Add garlic, crushed red pepper flakes, and salt. Cook about 1 hour. Check frequently to make sure the lentils don't burn.

Serve with basmati rice (see page 86).

Serves 6–8.

BASMATI RICE ⓟ

Basmati rice is known for its incredible fragrance. Combine with lentils to make a complete protein, excellent for a vegetarian or a family enjoying Indian food during the Nine Days.

6 cups water

2 teaspoons salt

4 teaspoons canola oil

3 cups uncooked basmati rice

Bring water to a boil. Add salt, oil, and rice. Bring to a boil again. Immediately reduce heat to a simmer. Cover and cook for 20 minutes. Do not lift lid while cooking. When finished, fluff rice and serve.

Serves 8–10.

SPECIAL BASMATI RICE ⓟ

A few simple additions makes this rice special.

6 cups cooked basmati rice (see above)

¼ cup raisins

½ cup frozen peas

¼ cup sliced almonds

Mix raisins, peas, and almonds into cooked rice.

Serves 8.

FRUIT CHUTNEY

This sweet and spicy side dish is served with an Indian meal. It complements the flavors of the food and is delicious in its own right as well.

8 apples, finely chopped

20 dried apricots

24 pitted prunes, quartered

3 small cloves garlic, chopped

1 cup apple cider vinegar

¼ teaspoon crushed red pepper flakes

1 teaspoon cinnamon

1 teaspoon powdered ginger

1 teaspoon cloves

2–3 cups sugar, to taste

Combine all ingredients in a large pot. Bring to a boil. Lower heat and simmer for 1 hour or until all fruit is soft. Stir frequently. Remove and chill.

Serve cold or at room temperature as an accompaniment to an Indian meal. Keep leftovers in a tightly covered container in the refrigerator. Keeps for 2 months in the refrigerator.

Serves 12.

SAMBALS

Sambals are wonderful additions to a traditional Indian meal. Choose as many or as few as you like.

¼ cup dried, shredded coconut

¼ cup raisins

¼ cup chopped apples

¼ cup chopped peanuts

¼ cup chopped almonds

¼ cup chopped green onions

Serve each sambal separately in a little bowl. Sprinkle them over curried chicken and rice.

Serves 6–8.

INDIAN

87

CHAI TEA D/D

A delicious sweet and spicy tea served hot or cold.

5 chai or rose chai tea bags

4 cups water

2 cups milk or soy milk

¼–½ cup sugar

cinnamon sticks, for garnish, optional

Bring water to a boil and pour into a tea pot. Add tea bags and steep for a few minutes. Add sugar and stir until it dissolves. Heat milk in the microwave or over a low flame and add to tea. Serve hot or cold with a cinnamon stick for garnish.

Serves 6–8.

Note: These are suggested proportions. Experiment until you create your own perfect combination.

INDEX